Parents
Listen

Parents
Listen

Lucienne Pickering

GEOFFREY
CHAPMAN

Uniform with this book

Boys Talk
Girls Talk

A Geoffrey Chapman book published by
Cassell Publishers Limited
Artillery House, Artillery Row
London SW1P 1RT
© 1981 Geoffrey Chapman, an imprint of Cassell Publishers
Limited

First published 1981
Reprinted with corrections 1984, 1986, 1988, 1989

British Library Cataloguing in Publication Data
Pickering, Lucienne
Parents listen.
1. Sex instruction
I. Title
612'.6007   HQ56
ISBN 0 225 66311 2

Diagrams by Illustra Design
Other illustrations by Alan Nivern

Printed and bound in Hungary

Contents

Introduction

Five children of my own has provided me with endless pleasure, some problems and plenty of practice in parenthood.

Fifteen years of counselling and a lifetime working with young people has enlarged my experience and given me many opportunities to pass it on to others.

No two people have the same life-experience, of course. There is no single blueprint for successful parenthood, just as there is no guaranteed trouble-free path of development from birth to adulthood. Nevertheless, *Parents Listen* has offered me the chance to distil some of what I have listened to and learned — I offer it in the hope that you, as parents or parents-to-be, may find something of yourself somewhere in these pages.

Working with young couples on pre-marriage courses has taught me never to assume that young people today are well informed on the subject of sex. They have vast resources in magazines, television and other media for learning about the *how* but very little about the *why*. The facts they acquire are often gathered like wild flowers wherever they can find them.

In schools there is still confusion. A well-organised science department arranges to give the biological information, but who helps the young people with the all-important matter of relationship? Quite rightly, they may look to families and especially parents to fill this in.

In good schools the pastoral teachers pick up what comes their way in the nature of relationships and reinforce what they optimistically hope is the ethic of the home. But in the home parents are losing confidence. Battered by the amount of sexual content in today's media, they find themselves robbed of the time they would like to enable their children's sexuality to evolve in a comfortable relationship with themselves.

Instead, young children are catapulted into a situation where factual information frequently overtakes any experience that the parents may have. Many parents have not even thought deeply about their own feelings on subjects like pre-marital intercourse, homosexuality and abortion. But the sophisticated *ten*-year-old is holding forth to his friends on these matters.

My work over the last twelve years with groups of parents has involved helping them through their own thinking, as well as focusing on their children. They have many anxieties about the pressures put on their children. They worry about their own ability to give the right answers, which shows how brainwashed by the media they have become. Loving and truthful answers were always around ever since parents first had babies.

I have found that parents who come to these discussions are deeply concerned. More than anything else they want their children to succeed in relationships. They want peace and love in their families. They are filled with joy when they see their youngsters enjoying good friendships, learning to relate to the adults in their lives, and becoming responsible members of the family. I share that feeling with them: it is as old as God's promise to Abraham.

In two companion books, *Girls Talk* and *Boys Talk*, I have attempted to put the necessary information into the context of family life.

Both books are written through the senses and feelings of the young person growing up. There is no specified age because there is no specified age. This growing-up business happens at various times with no special starting-place and rarely any ending since we learn continuously about relating to people.

It does not matter *when* you buy these books – it would be useful to read them yourself first. They set out a kind of pattern in the development of thinking and feeling which could be helpful to parents in understanding their child.

They are not fiction. Everything contained in both books is an accumulation of what I have learnt from boys and girls, plus what I have endeavoured to teach them during their school days and also as a counsellor. In spite of the dismal statistics we are bombarded with about divorce and battered babies and drop-out teenagers, happy families *do* exist.

In the formal coursework taught on the 'family' in schools, one of the set pieces is usually an essay on the ideal family. There is evidence in plenty that it exists for many children in their own home. They write of the love and care received from their parents, they express appreciation for the rules and discipline which they acknowledge as necessary, they wish to achieve the same success in their own future lives.

That is encouragement indeed for all my readers. You would not be buying and reading these books if you were not in that kind of bracket. In writing this book for parents, I have tried to keep in mind the questions and anxieties experienced by groups I have worked with — as well as the shared pleasures and responsibilities.

1
In the beginning

In the beginning was a baby. From the moment you held your baby in your arms – mother or father – you talked. You said loving words, you enveloped your baby in warmth and strength and security. You made skin-to-skin contact, holding the tiny darling against your face.

You loved him or her with your eyes, your smile, your mouth, your hands. You communicated. You gave that baby messages about the meaning of love.

The baby who has rested, loved and contented, in his parents' arms, will rest loved and contented in his lover's arms. Whatever sadnesses his life may bring, he will in the tenderest moment of love refer back to his sense of loving gained from you.

That is why my book begins with babies and not adolescents.

Most babies quickly become aware of mother and father. They know and recognise the voice, the touch, the feel and even the smell.

Very soon the baby gets messages from both parents about feeding, sleeping and playing.

He is expected to feed and expected to sleep. Hopefully there will be a playtime that seems to be mutually enjoyable, although for the baby he has to learn how, whereas the feeding and sleeping is a response to instinct.

At once you can see that the parent is also the teacher and the baby accepts both.

When the baby conforms to these patterns of feed, sleep, play, he is made to feel accepted and 'good' by the parents, so his happiness increases.

This feeling of happiness which comes from 'pleasing' parents is a very strong reflex built into your baby by you at a very early stage. If it is maintained all through the growing-up stage, it can become the means of guidance to the young adolescent and a better strength for you than admonishments or punishments.

Your baby quickly understands that not 'following' the rule produces frowns, anxiety and a different kind of voice. This little self-centred bundle, in a matter of weeks, is brought face to face with honest expressions and proper behaviour.

Most of the first year of his life is taken up with these 'lessons'. He learns to love, be loved, accept and be accepted. In doing that he also learns how to cope with frustration.

That may seem hard going for a little baby, but it is very important that he should meet frustration and deal with it successfully at this early age before he can analyse his situation, since very little justice exists in frustration and it is more important that he should regain his sense of 'being loved'.

One year old

From his second year onwards relationships get more complicated. He is still very concerned with himself and being loved, or with expressing his anger in any way he likes to experiment with. His interests, however, are concerned not just with feeding, but with eliminating the waste! It is about this time that parents embark upon the message of cleanliness and potty training.

He quickly learns that there is a proper time and place for this performance and that it is very important to his mother. Indeed he will offer his pot like a gift and receive words of love and praise in return.

This also brings a certain independence and sense of identity. It is one thing no one can make him do, so he is free to please his mother or withhold his gift as he likes.

How the mother deals with this situation is the subject of more books than a baby has nappies changed. A morning cup of coffee with young parents gave rise to this sort of conversation:

"How are you getting on with the potty training?"

"Oh, it's worse, if anything! Neil uses the pot every time and then saves some for his nappy afterwards!"

"Mine just refuses. She screams every time I take her near it."

"Samantha is quite good. If anything she's too bothered now and gets so upset, I have to comfort her every time she wets."

"Cathy enjoys it. She collects a smarty sweet for herself and she's cottoned on to sitting all her dolls on and collecting smarties for them."

"I don't think Kevin will ever get out of nappies – I get so worried about it that he simply can't relax and we've given up altogether and left it for a while."

There are lots of communications going on here between mother and baby, and all the messages are different. Lots of anxiety is being given to the baby and some rewards. But rewards may be sweets for doing what is expected of you, or loving words of comfort for not doing what is expected. It is all very confusing for a baby, and not a bad time for discovering what tempers are for.

Again, there are plenty of books for the subject to be pursued thoroughly enough. Its relevance here is only to show how we talk to our babies about body functions and how we convey important messages about them, perhaps with anxiety.

By the time you are achieving potty success, the little child has taken a long look at his relations. He now clearly sees himself as an individual, whereas before he felt slightly connected to mother. On becoming an individual, he is able to see his relationship with father, brothers and sisters if any, or with other members of the family like grandparents, uncles and aunts.

Not only is he sorting out how they relate to him, but he also has to accept that they have a relationship with each other.

We are all familiar with the toddler who squeezes himself between mother and father on the settee or walking out together. How many conversations between mother and father are wrecked by the banging of tables or shouting to come and see whatever is going on!

The child is telling you he doesn't want to share you, but he's not sure who the message is for. A little boy begins to feel his identity with daddy and a little girl with mummy.

At the same time you may get puzzled questions like "why haven't I a penis?" or "will she have one when she grows into a boy?".

13

"Why does daddy stand up when he goes to the toilet and mummy sit down?"

If you have read the girls' book, you will recall that Kate's little cousin asked similar questions. The little girl's father explained how she was different just because she is a girl and that one day she will grow into a woman like mummy and maybe have her own babies – then she will be a mother. But little boys grow into men like daddy and they become fathers.

For little children it is important to take only the simple questions they ask and give the simplest answer you can. However tempting may be the opportunity to embark on longer explanations or additional information, it will only confuse a small mind. When a child is confused about information, he has a nice little editing system which gets rid of it. Then your problem is that you think (not without some relief) that you have dealt with a particular piece of information, whereas the child has rejected it as too complicated.

At this age, little children say things like "when I grow up I shall marry you". They are very aware even then of the special relationship that exists between mother and father.

This is another opening for input like "when you grow up you will love someone else just like I love mummy/daddy, and you will want to marry him/her".

Or you can just laugh as though it was a great joke and this will introduce the idea to your child that this kind of talk about 'marrying' is not for him. It is a secret about which grown-ups laugh because only they know what the joke is.

That's not to say every answer is deadly serious: there is room for laughing about lots of our children's ideas – it is part of the fun of bringing up a family. But it is necessary, even essential, to give a serious answer as well, even if the question is unspoken.

Temper and truth

Jealousy is one of the new feelings experienced at this time and this makes a little child angry. Tantrums and temper are all he can show to express feelings that are not loving and good like hugging you.

Knowing and understanding these developments is not an excuse for parents to accept bad behaviour from their children. Instead, it is a lesson in dealing with ourselves and how the child is making us feel. It enables us to correct or rebuke or punish with a proper amount of disapproval, rather than a disproportionate amount of anger.

This is a 'parent lesson' offered by children to us if only we can learn from it. It holds good at every age in their lives. Far too much anger is saved up by parents from childhood and then heaped on the bewildered adolescent.

Long before your child is occupied with worries about starting school, he has absorbed from you the most important lessons about relationships. He has learnt how to please you, what kind of behaviour brings approval and acceptance. He knows what makes you angry and he knows when he feels angry. He has met frustration in many forms and if he does not always know how to deal with it, he has at least learnt that it passes in time and peace is restored to himself.

During this time he has also picked up some ideas about right or wrong. Not the right and wrong way of doing up the buttons on his woolly, but more difficult, abstract rights and wrongs. For instance, you mustn't hang onto the cat's tail even if it feels 'good' to you, and you mustn't eat the chocolates daddy bought mummy, even if you know she would give you one if she was in the room.

He does not always understand why these things are wrong and punishable, but he does know what effect they have on you. Since the natural basic need is always to be loved and accepted, he will accept your decision ultimately about the right and wrong, and he will conform to gain your approval.

Later as he grows up and develops in personality, he will test your decision more often. The value you have taught him as a child will still be there. The value is that of the 'relationship'. For this he can make sacrifices. For this he can give up some of his ideas, his possessiveness, and settle for more 'sharing', more giving-in and less self-assertion.

He learns this in the family, in the home, before any influence of school comes into his life. The payment for learning this is the growth of security.

In the girls' and boys' books, I have tied this security in with honesty because that is how friendships grow. It is also true of the parent-child relationship. It cannot grow without honesty. Honesty is essential for security. The little child must know that he can trust you, that you will show him by your feelings whether he is O.K. for you; and that if he asks you anything he will get a truthful answer.

2
Some early encounters

We have already looked at what is probably the earliest question of a child about his own body. During these same early years, a child may put to you any number of questions about babies, depending partly on his position in the family and partly on his natural curiosity.

The first child is likely to experience Mummy getting pregnant and new babies arriving. Hopefully the youngest in a family may gain these experiences from relatives or friends.

Certainly most little children at some time have asked where does the baby grow? How does it get in there? How does it get out? Or even embarrassed you at the shops by asking why someone is 'so fat'.

For a small child this kind of question is a direct and simple request for information. The shortest simple answer is the best. If you are anxious or want to explain it all in great detail, that is *your* problem: don't pass it on to your child!

"Where does the baby grow?"

"Inside mummy's tummy, in a special part for babies."

"How did it get in?"

"It grew from a tiny seed smaller than the ones you plant in the garden."

"How does it get out?"

"Through a special opening between the legs."

There are so many variations of the way a child puts questions that a book of ready-made answers has always seemed pretty useless to me. It is very rarely that we find ourselves sitting peacefully in the right surroundings, alone with our beloved child and facing the

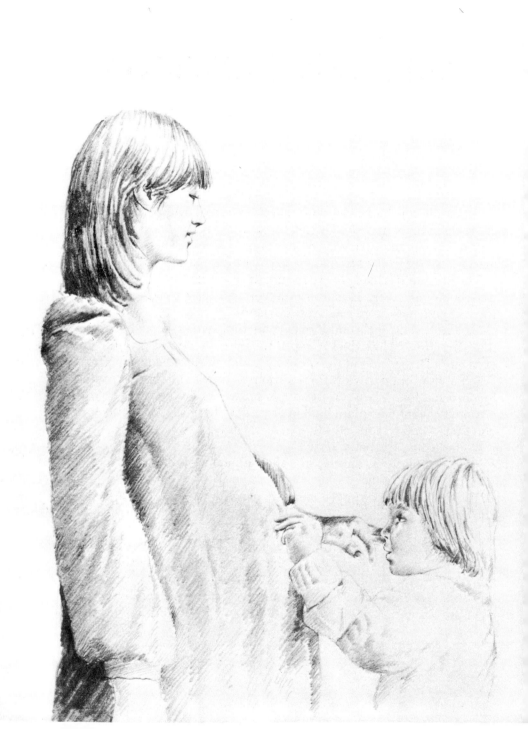

perfectly-phrased classic question. All too often we are in a super-market, or on top of a bus, or dishing up a meal for visitors, when the child offers his university challenge to us.

If it can be dealt with easily and quickly, do so. Otherwise say to the child, "I'm very busy just now, but I'll answer you later on when I'm putting you to bed. Don't forget to ask me." A child can accept that just as easily as father saying, "I'm busy with the car now, I'll help you in a few minutes."

The words to use

Many parents when talking in groups about sex education, have expressed difficulties about the proper names to the parts of the body. There are various reasons for the parents' difficulties and it is worth discussing this with your partner.

In the group discussions, it appears on the surface to be a matter of knowing how to pronounce 'foreign' words. Sometimes several minutes are spent talking about 'the words' before anyone can bring themselves to say 'breast' or 'penis' or 'vagina'.

Well, they *are* mostly 'foreign' words, Latin or Greek, as a rule. It is a pity we do not have English words that we are comfortable with. But 'breast' is a good English word and some people even stumble over that one. So perhaps not using proper names is a way of escaping from the job of talking truthfully and directly to the child about sex organs and their function.

If you talk to your partner about which words are important to use, it will not only help you decide together on one policy, but it will be a useful rehearsal to hear your own voice saying the words naturally to someone you are at ease with.

The first time I talked to a group of young children about babies, the word 'penis' did not come into my talk for quite a little while. When it did, the outlet of breath was actually audible. As though all the group had held their breath waiting to hear if I would say the word.

Now I use as many words as I need as soon as possible and then reinforce the knowledge by repeating them several times in the course of the discussion.

19

You have access to your child for much longer than a counsellor visiting the school. You can reinforce the knowledge at every opportunity and your child will feel at ease with the proper names.

Of course he will pick up nicknames and 'avoidance' names for various organs and functions, but at least he will know that what is used at home is the correct way to speak about these parts.

Who answers and when

The simple answer is, 'whoever is asked'. Most young couples who discuss this with me seem to be happy with the idea that a father or mother or person close to the child in affection would be the right person for this.

In practice it has often been the mother because she has been most often available to the child. This makes it appear to be the role of the mother to give sex education.

The pattern of family life is, however, changing very rapidly. Mother is not always the person most available. In some families father is very involved with the care of the small children. Mother may have a job in the evening and father takes over. Or grandma comes in during the day to look after the little ones.

From two years onwards they may spend mornings or days in play groups or pre-school groups. All this widens the possible circle of information. Parents may never be quite sure whether questions have been asked or answered. Neither can they be sure the right answers have been given or the right attitudes shown towards the subject.

This is a good reason for checking out now and then by discussing the day with the little child. A very good rule is for father or mother to have a special talking time and to arrange this at the same time each day.

When the child is quite small, bedtime seems to be the best time for a chat. Most parents institute a story time with their children and this would seem to be a good time for talking about how the day went and what new things they have learnt or seen.

Try to avoid the academic learning because it narrows the view of a child about learning. Encourage the idea that just being with people is learning, going for walks is learning, playing a game is learning.

Once the child gets the idea you can explore feelings much more easily.

"I bet daddy (or mummy) was surprised you could put your own pyjamas on."

"I expect Miss J (at the nursery) was quite sad the little gerbil died?"

"Did you notice that the honeysuckle is open by the kitchen door? Have a look tomorrow."

It seems so obvious, doesn't it? And yet surprisingly enough we have to make a much more conscious effort at these things than our grandparents did.

Why? Probably very much to do with the changing pattern in our home life. Something about the speed with which each day is lived. There is so much urgency to get on with the next job, that the child is at risk of becoming a 'next job', as if he was someone to hurry off to school or to the baby-minder or to bed because there is so much else to be done.

Our own time is so full of organisation that we have difficulty in giving ourselves permission to sit down and relax. We used to hear people say 'time costs nothing to give someone'. Nowadays it seems to cost us quite a lot – not in money so much as in effort and self-giving. Nevertheless, it is the most important, the most valuable gift we can give to our children.

During one whole year I worked every week with eleven-year-olds in small discussion groups. During that time we examined many feelings, such as being the 'oldest' or the 'youngest' or the only girl or boy. At some stage with each group I asked the question "when were you most happy?" and "What can you recall from your earliest memories as the happiest time in your life?"

I expected holidays, birthdays and Christmas to figure largely. Not at all! It was storytime with mum or dad before going to bed. With hardly any exception, every group recounted vividly the pleasures of this time they had alone with a parent. It seemed to be the private, individual attention of mother or father that they valued so highly.

This special time ought to be available to our children for as long as they need it – probably until they are young adults. Even after they are married you will find that if the habit has been formed in youth they will seek you out for all kinds of little domestic talks or family worries.

Sometimes the relief of finding that the older child in a family is able to wash and get ready for bed by himself changes the pattern. We move on to the needs of the younger one(s) and give praise to the independence of the older child.

When that happens you have lost a good ally. Your oldest child is always the best ambassador you have in the family. All that you can give them in talk and consideration and attention will be an investment which will pay dividends in the other children.

22

Certainly give plenty of praise for all signs of independence, but it is still possible to retain the link with the bedtime routine by saying something like "you can have ten minutes with a book and then I'll be up to say goodnight." Or just remind them to call out when they are in bed because you like coming up to say goodnight.

This will still give you a chance to have a little chat about anything you or they may choose. Very often there is not much that is special in the discussion. So often in fact, that you may be tempted to think the habit is 'grown out of' or of very little use. But if you collect some little anxiety of theirs about school, or a friend, or something they are going to do in the next few days, then it is really worthwhile. And it is only because you patiently give this time that they feel able to share these anxieties.

It is equally important to hear what they say about the happy things and indeed just to hear what they say. Listening to our children is a special kind of art. They often don't say the obvious things that help us to make the right answer. They may approach things from a roundabout rather than a straight road. For example, this is a conversation with a four-year-old:

"Only very old people die, don't they?"
"Usually, but sometimes people die from illness or accidents."
"But they would still be old?"
"Not always – why do you ask?"
"Are you old enough to die?"
"I hope I shall be around a long time and watch you grow into a man. What made you think about me dying?"
"Well I just want to know who will do up my shoelaces if you aren't there."

By such circuitous routes the child comes to a simple problem of the moment. He could just as easily have begun with shoelaces and ended exploring the idea of death.

Death is often as big a mystery as life and birth to a child. Whereas we know quite a lot about birth and can give quite a few facts about this to our young inquisitors, we know very little about death, its moment of happening or the experience. When it occurs in the family it should be talked about with the child. The imaginings of a child's mind are worse than any reality.

23

Fear comes from whispered unknowns and unfortunately both the subject of birth and the subject of death are frequently dealt with in hushed and mysterious voices.

If our children are to experience the richness of a fully human life, then they must be allowed grief as well as joy. They can only gain permission to weep tears of grief if you yourself can show sadness. The 'stiff upper lip' has been the cause of many young people being unable to make warm and loving relationships later in their lives.

3
The young child at school

Once your child starts on his or her school career, you can no longer control the circle of his friends or the sources of his information. This may at first thought seem frightening. In fact, however, it can be a wider means of learning for the child and of help for the parent.

Consider first the child who has become used to talking about anything and everything with his parents. He is still going to continue in this habit because this is the way you have taught him, the way that brings closeness and understanding with the person he loves most. You will be listening and hearing all his messages and the right times will present themselves for correcting or adding to his information.

What happens if, in spite of all the time you give your child including his own 'special' time, he has never asked questions about babies or bodies? Some children just don't get curious about these things. They may be wholly occupied with learning about books or toys or how the house runs. There are limits to what the young mind can assimilate.

Or he may not have had the stimulus for asking such questions: a boy may only have brothers, or a girl sisters and so neither will be very curious about the other sex. The child may be an only child or he may belong in a one-parent family so that there are not enough relationships going or 'visual aids' to stimulate interest.

For all these reasons, school is going to prove a great help to the parents and the child. He or she will encounter here whatever relationship they have missed out on at home.

Most primary schools today encourage some interest in the rearing of small animals. The children delight in caring for gerbils, mice, guinea pigs and rabbits. They view mating as a very matter-of-fact necessity so that they can enjoy the birth of the young offspring.

I have never heard a young child question why animals mate. They may ask "what is he doing?" but they accept at once that this is necessary if you are to have young gerbils or rabbits or whatever. It is at that same level of interest that the young child asks how a baby gets inside a mother.

By the time your child is in school, he needs more than the simple toddler's answer about the baby growing from a seed. You have to take the opportunity of explaining that a baby has a mother and a father and that neither can make a baby alone.

When the opportunity comes for explaining this, it is well worth taking it. As the child moves on from seven years to ten years old, his questions become more difficult for you to explain and less simple for him to understand.

Between five and seven years old the child is still very interested in an objective way about the facts of reproduction.

Explain first that it is the joining together of the sperm from the father (or life-cell if you prefer that term) with the egg or life-cell of the mother that makes a baby. This is the only way for human beings to create a new life.

Then use a little diagram to show him where the egg is in the mother and where the father's sperm enters and travels to meet the

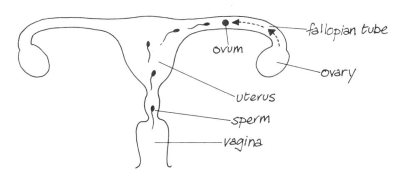

egg. If you describe it without a picture you can tell him to think about a pear held so that the stalk hangs down. This is just about the size of the womb in a woman, which is the place where a baby grows.

The stalk is like the passage into the womb — it is called a vagina. When the sperm meets an egg they join together and fasten to the side of the womb. There it will stay and grow and feed and move for nine months until the baby is strong enough to be born and live outside in the world.

When the father and mother want a baby, the father will put his penis in the vagina of the mother and that way he can send the sperm into the womb. This is a very special way that mothers and fathers have for loving each other. That is why they love their babies so much, because they made the baby in this special loving way.

It is only when your child is so young and uncomplicated that you can easily give this message of special love. That is why it is important to take any opportunity at an early age to explain it.

As the child grows older, he is going to meet all kinds of attitudes and facts which will confuse this message for him if he has not received it early in life. Building on a positive basis of a man and a woman's love for each other makes it easier to explain the situations he will meet later in life.

It is a good rule, when talking to any child or young person about relationships, to start with the normal, the positive and the good because they are, in fact, in the majority.

When you have explained the normal sexual relationship in various contexts during the early years of a child's life, it becomes easier for him to accept that some people may choose another way of living their lives. They have this right to choose because they are free people. But in our kind of community the usual pattern is for a man and woman to love one another, to marry, and to share the responsibility of bringing up children.

Some ways of introducing the subject

It may be that your child has now settled into school life, is approaching his first year in juniors and is still not giving you openings to help his understanding of the simple basic facts about reproduction.

Do not be too anxious. Many small children from a loving family have an innate acceptance of the fact that they grew out of this loving situation. He is still absorbing the lessons of sexuality and good relationships, but has not become interested in the technical details.

Every small child learns either at home or at school about the Christmas story. The first introduction into the mysteries of drama will probably be through some form of Nativity play.

This affords parents a good opportunity for exploring the subject of birth. The angel telling Mary gives you an opportunity of explaining how that was special because it was a message from God. Usually mothers and fathers tell each other about these things. They usually decide when they want a baby and plan it themselves.

Little children themselves act out how tired Mary was when she came to Bethlehem because the baby was to be born. Again you can explain how worried Joseph would have been, at the same time showing how simple and natural birth is because they managed in such a simple surrounding.

They are not all of the child's unspoken questions, but at least you will have established two important facts. One is that it is a subject you like talking to him about, and the other is that it must be a good thing since it can be talked about in connection with people like Mary, Jesus and God.

We have already mentioned the possibility of the child learning about mating from pets kept at school or at home. This is another opportunity not to be missed. On the other hand if you are concerned with giving your child a special value for the meaning of sexual love in humans, this is the time to do so.

Unless you explore this mating of animals with your child, he may make, or allow the school to make, a logical deduction like 'that is what humans do'. And the whole thing becomes lost in a general umbrella statement which constitutes sex education for the school and relief for you that 'it' is now over.

There are some important points to make even to small children about relationships in this area. Humans are different from animals because they have a free will to choose who they will marry, and they have the ability to love. They are also the only living creatures who know how a baby is conceived and born. For all other kinds of animal, birth 'happens': it is neither planned nor understood. It is a natural consequence of a response to instinct.

Mating is part of this same response. There is no meeting as humans do with a progression through friendship to a deep love and a promise made to each other to care for and share everything.

Time spent in the early years teaching these simple truths about people will make all the difference to the young adult when he is exposed to suggestions from outside influences that sex is just another game we play in the search for fun.

When I have discussed these truths with youngsters in junior school, they have been very interested in this idea that they understand about human love and birth. They see it as good evidence that they are different from animals.

Of course, they defend strongly the belief that animals love – which they do, in a limited way. The child needs to look at how 'love' is understood in a family – what caring and sharing is about and how we make sacrifices for each other. We can express love in many more ways than an animal. For example, we can 'think' about people we love and plan to do something for them.

Another approach at this age may be through a newly-awakened curiosity in their bodies. Because they are now in school with other girls and boys, children from one-sex families may suddenly become aware of the difference between one sex and the other. It is often a rather silly, giggly stage when undressing for P.E. becomes a peep show and the word 'knickers' sends them into convulsions.

Some of this of course is just nonsense that passes, but if you are still sitting on a hot seat waiting for your youngster to ask questions, then by all means make use of this new opening.

Enjoy the laughs with them, but at the same time introduce a few of your own questions like "didn't you know little girls don't have a penis? That's how their mummies knew they were little girls. That's how I knew you were a little boy."

Tell him a girl has a vagina. Tell him when she's grown up she will be able to have babies and when he grows he will be able to be a father, for that is what these different parts of their bodies are for.

If he doesn't want to go any farther with the talk, it doesn't matter. If he doesn't seem interested, it doesn't matter. All that matters all the time is that your children hear you say these words and talk in an ordinary friendly voice about these matters.

By seven years of age, a child can begin to get ideas from other children that 'sex' is a taboo subject. It's a grown-ups' secret and you get into trouble if you talk about it. They may even pick up ideas about it being dirty because all too often these words are used in connection with the sex organs.

Little boys may sometimes handle their penis or little girls their vagina almost idly whilst reading or looking at television. I have noticed infant classes at school sitting cross-legged on the floor at story time, and some little children will pat themselves in these places almost like a baby rocks himself to sleep. They are not significant habits and will soon be lost in the busy day's work. They are more of a comfort-thing like thumbsucking.

When a child sits reading and sucking his fingers, a parent will often gently pull away the hand without saying anything. Or he may say, "Your mouth will get sore if you pull at it all the time." It is strange that parents find it hard to bring that same calm behaviour to the other situations. All too often the child is rebuked with words like "That's dirty!" or "Don't be rude!", or even "I'll smack you if you touch yourself". Enough of that kind of admonishment will certainly give a child feelings of guilt and 'not nice' attitudes about his sex organs.

Unfortunately, even when you contrive as parents to have positive approaches to these matters, you still have other family and school pressures to contend with. The same punitive words can be implanted in a child by well-meaning but old-fashioned aunts, relatives or teachers.

The only way to counteract this — since you cannot know when it happens — is to be sure you give your child strong positive messages about himself or herself and how nice it is being a boy or a girl.

The Father and Mother role

A lot of talk goes on today about the changing role of parents and women's liberation. They are often confused by the media as well as the masses.

A child needs a very positive idea about the role of a father and that of a mother. A boy must recognise himself in the father and the girl in the mother.

As children grow older they will want to be quite different persons — that is the struggle of adolescence. But first they must find some identity with the parents in order to gain their own independence and self-identity.

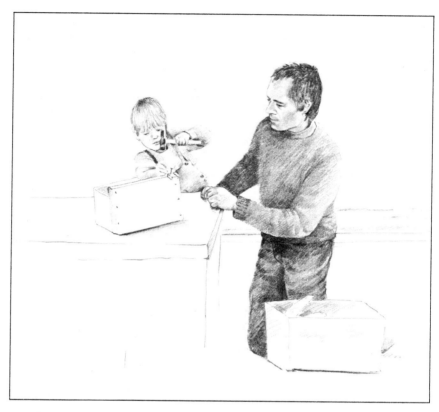

The equality of status in the family is quite different from equality of role. The child can only benefit from examples of sharing work and problems and pleasures in the home. It is not important to him whether daddy or mummy changes the nappy or baths him at bedtime, just so long as he clearly enjoys the different experience and recognises the person giving it to him as father or mother.

Each parent will bring their own manner to the task and the child will enjoy being fussed and cuddled by mum or having a rough and tumble with dad.

A little boy quickly learns that he must be gentle with mum; she doesn't take kindly to thumps in the chest or hair being pulled. He begins to understand that there is a way to win his mother with cuddles and delight his father with fisticuffs.

On the other hand the little girl of seven or eight can be quite a flirt. She knows just how to coax daddy and enchant him and she also recognises that her mother knows this about her, because her mother is a woman, so she realises she has really lost the battle for dad and it's only a game. From her mother she can gain her sense of womanliness. They enter into a conspiracy about all kinds of things in the home. From her father she gets a sense of femininity, and begins all kinds of awarenesses of his strength and gentleness, his attraction and excitement.

Loving parents, fulfilling their roles, awaken the sexuality of their child's nature slowly. It unfolds like a bud into flower. It thrives in the sunshine of love and the fresh air of truth.

4
The junior school and sex education

In *Boys Talk* you will see that at one stage in their development, they refer to the film they saw in primary school about sex education.

One of them found it difficult to follow, "full of 'long words'," he said. The others had not seen a film in primary school and were anticipating – a little anxiously – the lesson in which it would be shown in secondary school.

There is still quite a divergence of opinion among parents and schools about the best time for introducing talks and films on sex education. There are even quite a large number of parents who think that schools should not tackle this subject at all.

Most of these differing opinions show underlying anxieties about the age and maturity of the children, the effect upon their imagination, the outcome of the lessons and a sense of inadequacy in parents to cope with this task.

Before discussing *how* the subject is dealt with in schools, we should look at some of the reasons *why* schools are concerned with it.

In the many years I have spent discussing this project with teachers, I have never encountered anyone who thought that they could do this job better than a parent: indeed, few wished to participate at all in this part of a child's education. So there is no evidence that teachers wish to usurp the role of a parent.

There is, however, much anxiety among teachers that children are not being adequately helped in these matters by their parents. The reasons for this are numerous and varied. Parents themselves have frequently not received any teaching from their parents and have picked up their information in random ways. This does not mean they do not wish to do better for their children, but it does mean that without help they may not know how or what to teach them.

I have already said that the most important lesson is in the living example of a married relationship. Nevertheless, because of the way a child is bombarded with sex from the outside world, it is necessary to give much more correct, detailed, factual material to them as they are growing up.

What most schools are saying is that it is a partnership. They have the skills for breaking down knowledge to the relevant level of each child. The parents have the charisma necessary to put the knowledge into its proper context.

Within the classroom a teacher is exposed for five hours a day to these young children. Every facet of the child is presented at some time to the teacher. Many relationships in the classroom and many conversations arising from them may never be presented in the home. A teacher must have the confidence to pick up and use whatever is offered.

Parents cannot wear blinkers about this subject. It is not just going to be talked about at home as if by magic. It is therefore better if parents can discuss this subject with the teachers and enter into a partnership over it.

Indeed, if the child is at a school which never seems to mention the subject, a parent should at least enquire what provision is being made for sex education. It may be that the whole subject is so well integrated into the curriculum that the school no longer feels the need to consult with parents. This is probably the most natural way of teaching the subject.

On the other hand, the school may not wish to become involved in such matters and it will then be at the parents' request that the possibility of instruction in this area may be considered.

Certainly the best way of ensuring that it is dealt with to your satisfaction, is for you to ask questions about how it is done. Very few schools embark on this kind of programme without consultation with parents. In fact, they may offer help to the parents in dealing with the subject or they may suggest that they work directly with the children.

It is at such consultations that I have become involved with groups of parents and learnt about their worries. The most frequently expressed anxiety is about the right age. There never seems to be a right answer to this, simply because children vary so much in maturity and the degree of exposure they have to information in the home.

The discussion about right age may indeed be a valid one of maturity or it may be an escape from the pressure of dealing with the task. If it is a matter of age, then I can only contribute my experience with young children between seven and twelve years in primary schools. When a child does not understand either the film or the discussion, he 'cuts out'. He uses the editing mechanism I have already mentioned and picks up only what he is willing and able to understand.

A group of seven year olds watched the B.B.C. film 'Where do babies come from'. One little boy's only comment was "I liked the horse!" A little girl said, "My mum's got a nightdress like that". For these two children it was all that they recognised. For others, questions were legion.

If you have already established easy communication with your child on these matters, you have no problem. They will tell you what they remember, ask you what they didn't understand and endorse everything they have already learnt. In fact, all that the school does is prove to your child how absolutely right his parents are.

If your child is one of the non-starters, then the film or lesson will stimulate his questions and give you an opportunity to show your willingness to discuss the subject.

Perhaps you are keen to help your child, but quite unable to do so because you recognise your own difficulty with the subject. In that case the school can only be of help to you, indeed your only hope.

If you belong to the ever-decreasing minority who think children should not be told anything, then you are not likely to be reading this book anyway.

After the matter of the right age, the discussion usually moves to content. Parents are divided again on how much a child of this or that age should be told. Some think only about the baby growing inside the mother. Others think everything should be told. Some do not want intercourse described.

The difficulty here is that we cannot control the children's questions. They take us as far as they want to go. In a group of ten year olds I have had questions from boys about 'periods', masturbation, abortion and contraception. Girls have asked about birth, caesarian section, twins, handicapped children. It is quite incredible how much they pick up from television, magazines and adults' conversations. Gone are the days when 'midwife' was the whispered pearl of wisdom passed around a class. Nowadays, they even tease each other about being 'homos'.

It is probably fair for you to assume that teachers are only going to deal with what the child offers as his question. They are not going to offer details, or information that is not asked for. In that, they echo your own attitudes, namely, treat each child and each question as individual and serious.

I have already said that schools will only embark on this after consultation with parents. If it is already a part of their curriculum, you will become aware of this before your child starts at the school. Otherwise you will receive some notification regarding the introduction of the project into their work.

It is a very good idea to use this time to check up with your child where he is in this subject. The school affords you a good opportunity

37

for re-opening what may have become a closed subject, and also of offering a book at this stage for reference, so that he or she may check up at any time without having to ask you.

Most schools use films like 'Where do babies come from', 'Living and growing' and 'Merry-go-round'. They are all very carefully designed by experts in child education. They can never replace what you give in the home. At best, they are only an aid to your own 'home tuition'.

Your experience, as parents, will have shown you how many times you find yourself re-stating in many different ways the same kind of lesson. It begins with "say 'thank you' " and goes on into adolescence with reminders like "don't forget to send a thank-you letter to Auntie". Sex education is not different. It begins simply and early, and continues into adolescence accumulating more facts, more attitudes and more wisdom as it grows.

The school, then, is but a small fragment of this pattern and the extension must be from the home. By the time your child is ready to transfer to secondary education he or she should be at ease with the whole subject of sex. You will have established your lines of communication and our young student will be well on the way to understanding what you call values and relationships.

If, for any reason, this form of communication has not been started, it is unlikely that your child will raise with you the subject of sexual relationships and related information after this age.

This is because the development of adolescence involves the growing awareness of feelings and sexuality. The young teenager is less objective about the facts of sex and reproduction. He no longer has a child-like curiosity about 'how'. The whole subject becomes a personal involvement which he would find embarrassing to reveal to a person as close to him as a parent.

In this case the school is again your most valuable ally. Almost certainly information will be given in the biology curriculum and probably relationships will be developed in the pastoral side of schooling.

You will find in *Boys Talk* and *Girls Talk* how the young people were listened to and helped by caring teachers. Each of their questions was dealt with seriously, and although the answers in the book are condensed, they arose out of quite a lot of discussion in the group.

In addition, *Girls Talk* shows Kate talking a great deal to her young aunt while in the boys' book Andy talks to his brother-in-law. It is good for young people to have friendships like these outside of the family. Often when your own emotional involvement is too strong for you to receive a young person's anger or worry, it is better for them to find a more neutral ground on which to sort out their feelings.

It does not mean necessarily that you have failed to communicate: it often means that a young person wants to believe his parents and therefore seeks confirmation from other people whose opinion he values, so that he feels reassured that he is thinking 'on the right lines'.

5
Adolescence

For most children this is likely to begin in their secondary stage of education. For parents it signifies a change in attitude towards them as a 'supreme' authority, and a change in the young person from the objective consideration of sexuality to the subjective.

So far as factual information is concerned, it is now mainly in the hands of the school. There will be two main sources of input: through the science department and through the peer group.

Whether your child communicates well with you, or not at all, you will still receive through your child whatever information he is getting. You need to know how to recognise it. It is a great deal more subtle in the adolescent than in the young child.

Menstruation

Some girls develop very early in life and may start to menstruate – or have 'periods' – whilst they are still in primary school. If that is the case for your daughter, then all that follows here is just as relevant since her early maturity will be matched by her understanding of the situation.

Most girls begin their periods between twelve and fourteen years of age, some may be later and some earlier; the timing is not a cause for anxiety. If there is no sign of this happening by sixteen years of age, you would do well to seek medical advice. However, your own daughter would probably be so aware of this fact that she would ask to see a doctor.

Periods are something young girls talk about together quite a lot and often have a little apprehension, however well prepared they have been at home.

At first they view the few who have started with some curiosity, but gradually, as more join the ranks, those who are waiting grow more anxious. It is a good thing to be aware of this and to reassure your child from time to time.

Most of the worries are very simple things which, in the course of our well-prepared instruction on the subject of why and how, we tend to overlook. Girls ask me, "how do I put on a sanitary towel?" "What will happen if I'm in assembly when it starts?" "Do people notice when you are unwell?"

You can reassure your daughter on the first point by giving her a pad, showing her how it loops onto a belt or sticks onto her pants. Buy her her own packet and leave them in her room so that she feels some independence and senses your confidence in her to manage herself. Suggest she carries one well-wrapped in clean polythene at the bottom of her school bag, so that she is prepared, and afterwards to have one with her about the time that she expects to start again.

Tell her there are always towels available in school; she can go to the office, or the school nurse, or even ask her own teacher. It is so normal and ordinary that no one minds being asked and everyone in school — both men and women teachers — knows about periods.

The worry about when it happens is because girls tell me they think it will be a great rush of blood that they cannot stop. They are always very relieved when they discover it will only be a few drops, enough to stain their pants a little. Often they can wait until they go home and tell their mothers, but if they are prepared with a towel at hand, all the better.

No one is going to notice this unless they wish to broadcast it to all around them. It is an opportunity to reinforce our teaching on discretion.

Most young people from about ten years onwards have started developing their own ideas about modesty and decorum. It will partly come from within them and partly from the way they are brought up. Each family has its own code of behaviour on the subject of nudity. If you are at ease with the idea of being seen undressed by your children, they will probably be equally at ease with one another.

However, it is my interesting experience that at some unspecified stage in growing up, children will suddenly say "you could have knocked on the door before you came in". It must be at that moment that Eve picked the first fig-leaf!

On the other hand, if wandering around the house in the nude is just 'not you' then it would be ridiculous to do so in a self-conscious fashion just because you read an article in a magazine.

The essential, as always, is to be natural: to be totally at ease with yourself and your children. They have special little 'antennae' that register immediately if they think they have caught you being embarrassed.

That is why on the subject of periods we may take an opportunity of saying again that these things to do with our personal lives are only really of interest to us and maybe to close friends or family, but not really for general announcement.

The notion put forward by some girls of being 'unwell' is quite common and, regrettably, is a relic from the past. It is in fact quite 'well' to be having periods and quite a normal function of our bodies. It may also come from the fact that some people experience discomfort at the beginning of a period. The girl concerned may have seen a mother or sister lying down at this time and picked up the notion that they are ill.

If you do have back-ache or cramp or such discomforts, it certainly is unpleasant. Some young girls have quite a bad first day and look very waxen and drawn. It is not the general case for everyone and your young daughter needs reassurance, not added anxieties. Encourage her to think of periods as a normal occurrence that does not have to change any of her normal routine.

There is a hidden bonus here for the parents of daughters. You may not have been able, for any of the reasons already stated, to have talked to your child about the facts of reproduction and about our sexual functions. Here is your last opportunity to open up this line of communication.

Depending on how naturally and easily you can cover the information you can regain a lot of lost ground here. At this stage, and with menstruation only a few months away, your daughter can take quite a lot of information in. You will find it easier to explain with diagrams: this is always so, simply because it removes you from the focus of the listener.

Allow her plenty of time for questions; don't hurry the time you have given her. Show her by your manner that this interests you as well as her and that it is a subject about which she may often wish to ask further questions in the next few years. It will please you if she does want you to be of help to her always.

I would like to put in a special plea here for fathers to become involved. It is very important – and also very rewarding – to show your daughter at this stage that you recognise her 'initiation' into womanhood. There is no way that I can overestimate the value of this shared moment in their lives. If you read Kate's Diary in *Girls*

Talk, you will see that her father made a hidden reference to this and how 'special' and important she felt because of it. A little gift like chocolates or flowers would be a memorable way of marking the occasion, but even little jokes about extra pocket money are very acceptable.

Too many girls have told me how depressing the event seems. Mothers say "poor thing" and friends say "hard luck". The whole idea seems shrouded in gloom and all too often it is still referred to as "the curse". This colours the whole attitude towards womanhood and motherhood. It is little wonder, then, if girls grow up dreading the event and feeling ill when it arrives. They carry the whole attitude with them into marriage and I have even heard young husbands speak gloomily of this monthly trial they have to bear with their wives.

Therefore, Christian folk, rejoice! This is the threshold of womanhood, the promise of fulfilment, the hope of future generations!

One of the lads

It may be that your son comes out with some remark like "girls are soft, they're always getting out of swimming just because they don't like getting wet and cold. We're not allowed to miss swimming ever, it's not fair." This is the kind of opportunity you need to check out or put in more information.

You may have done quite a good job on his performance in growing up, but you may have missed out on his knowledge of the opposite sex. He himself may have cut out that bit of information as being irrelevant at the time he received it.

It's worth a casual "They may be having a period". This will give him the opportunity to ask you what you mean or to reflect on his own attitude or to look it up in his book.

Whether you have one or more children, one sex or both, and however well you have briefed them, they should by now own a good reliable book to which they may make reference whenever they wish. One of the distinctive features of adolescence is a need for privacy and independence and 'looking things up' achieves this.

45

It is a good idea at this age to go through some of the explanations again as the chance arises. Reinforcement and repetition are the basis of all learning.

You can explain with a diagram like this:

The journey of the unfertilised egg

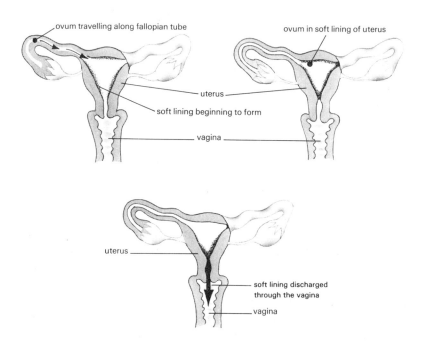

Show them how the ovum comes down into the womb, the lining grows to protect it, but the ovum is not fertilised so it dies and disintegrates. Ask them if that's how it is explained at school and get them to tell you how the teacher explained it to them. The more often you exchange the words the better for talking.

Girls at this stage, especially if they go to a mixed school, may want to know about boys' development – do they have anything like periods?

Ideally it would be good if the family could talk together about these differences, but it does not often happen that brothers and sisters have the same questions at the same time. This is partly because they differ in age of development. Boys are usually a year or so later than a girl in coming to puberty.

It becomes fairly apparent to a boy that girls begin to grow breasts and develop a figure – boys are less likely to come home with questions about this, more likely to express admiration, certainly interest.

This is something of a revelation to fathers. Suddenly they are being taken into a confederacy. Their sons are seeking to be acknowledged as man to man on the subject of good-lookers. It is a pity if

fathers put them down with remarks like "you're too young to be talking like that". It will stop the flow of confidence later in his teens.

It is less obvious to the girl that changes are taking place in a boy and the opportunity should be taken somewhere at this age to explain to her about 'wet dreams' and how the sperm is collected in the testicles. She should know about erections and understand why and how. All this is as matter of fact to a boy as her own development and menstruation is to her. No special weight is attached to any of this information, which should be explained in simple biological terms. Reference can again be made to the girls' or boys' book: explanations are given in both books.

Girls will notice a boy's voice breaking and of course eventually she will be aware that he needs to shave occasionally. She should know that a boy is as embarrassed about these developments as she is when teased about her figure.

The voice in particular is a worry to many young boys. They tell me that because it is 'broken' and uneven in pitch it tends to come out in noisy jerks, especially if they are upset or angry. Parents, they tell me, frequently accuse them of being too abrupt and bad-tempered when all that happens is the words are blurted out in varying pitches that they cannot control.

It has certainly been my experience in discussion groups that the more excited they get the less control there is of the voice and it frequently sounds very sharp and aggressive.

Girls on the other hand are less in control of their tears at this time. However hard they try to master this, they will invariably show anger or frustration by crying.

Parents need to be aware of both these difficulties of adolescence and to show some acceptance and tolerance.

6
Friendships

You will recall that the peer group is one of the two sources of information now available to your teenager — besides the home.

Because parents know this they are anxious for their children to make the 'right kind' of friends. It is one of the few areas however over which we have no control. We choose our own friends. It is something no one can impose on us. Like love, it is freely chosen and freely given.

During adolescence a young person will change friends quite often. Friends at this time in their life fill all kinds of needs for them. They are important because they help the young person to know himself, and also paradoxically to forget himself.

At this time, while they are changing emotionally as well as physically, their personality becomes fragmented like a broken mirror. A part is reflected in each piece and they all have to be put together to see the whole person.

Each friend may see only one part of the whole person. Even parents see different sides of their child's personality, but they are never too sure which is the real one. You can become as confused about who your child is as the child is himself.

If you do pick up this very confused feeling and if it makes you wonder just what sort of adult your son or daughter will become, be glad of this awareness. Use it to understand better what is going on in the teenager. He too is unsure who he is or how he will grow up.

Who are these friends he chooses?

According to which part of his personality is more dominant at the time, so will he choose his friends. If he feels in need of sympathy, understanding, the attraction will be for older boys or girls, or even for teachers or friends in the family.

On the other hand as he − or she of course − grows more secure in their relationships, they may feel able to take on younger friends or people their own age who may be more disadvantaged than them. They experience the value of giving their own strengths of sympathy and understanding to others.

They may go through several friendships with shy retiring people that make them feel strong and confident; or they may fasten onto strong leader characters and take refuge in their group organisation.

Eventually these various aspects of character become less polarised; they are brought together in the finding of friends who are complementary to them and share similar interests, but who stimulate the best qualities in them.

It requires patience and love to bear with them in all these trials. It

is useless to attempt guidance. If the talk is good between you then your son or daughter may sound you out on your opinions about some of these people. It is wise to test the ice before stepping on it.

When discussing these friendships with groups of 13/14-year-olds they frequently put the situation into a role play to show me what happens at home. This is the kind of thing that happens:

"Mum, can I go out tonight?"
"Where to?"
"Just the disco."
"Who with?"
"Oh, a gang of us."
"I'm not sure I like the gang you go with."
"You don't know them."
"I don't want to."
"That's typical, you're just prejudiced."
"I just know that you get ruder every day since you went with them."

(It could just as easily be 'the way you speak', 'the way you dress', 'the hours you keep' or 'the swearing you've started'.)

These are all typical parental complaints against some choices of friends. It is quite justifiable from a parent's point of view. It probably *is* the group who is promoting the change of attitude. On the other hand the young person is testing himself and his behaviour against his only frame of reference – the code of his own home.

It is not an invitation for you to agree with your son or daughter; it is a request for you to re-state your standards. This is much more effective when expressed that way than put into the negative form of criticising his friends.

Feedback from these same youngsters on how criticism of friends affects them, is like this:

"I feel as though dad's saying there's only one way of doing things and that's his. It makes me angry."
"It's like saying you don't know how to choose friends I have to do it for you. I get mad at that."
"Mum makes out she has to blame someone else for what I do, why can't she let me be bad sometimes. I can't always be as perfect as she wants."
"I just get so cross I do the opposite of what they want."

52

When we change the role play and make the parent say what they feel about this, we get:

"I feel anxious in case my child is going wrong."
"I feel afraid that I can't control the changes."
"I feel disappointed that they have rejected my standards."
"I'm afraid she'll get pregnant."

Here we have the young person understanding the parents' attitudes even though he/she is too young to know how to use that understanding.

Parents should be mature enough to know how to use their understanding and they can always check it out by saying, "I suppose you think I'm always blaming your friends?"

It isn't easy to make communication at this kind of level with adolescents. Some have enough insight to work on the subject but

some (both parent and child) have too much anger and feeling to think at this cool level. Some young adolescents are like hedgehogs, they go into a tight ball and put out all their prickles and you can't get near them.

In any one family you have a variety of personality and behaviour patterns with each young person. Monitoring the first child through adolescence does not, unfortunately, give you a blueprint for the others.

Kate in *Girls Talk* is a very perceptive young person but even she gets into a row with dad about being home late. All the things she says about being old-fashioned, too strict, not understanding, all her shows of rebellion are familiar facets of growing up.

Old-fashioned

Most young people accuse their parents of being old-fashioned when they come into conflict with them. That in itself is significant since the intention is to use it as a weapon when it will hurt most. Very rarely, for instance, do teenagers bother calling their grandparents old-fashioned. They know they are. So this is an accusation made to solicit favour for some permission or possession that they wish to acquire. It is highly manipulative because you wish to refute the implication without losing your sense of values.

If it was just to do with clothing, it would be a simple issue. It is quite true that you don't always like their choice of clothes, or their music. There is something to be said for their argument that they don't want you to like it; they just want you to accept their liking. All too often, parents criticise the young person and it is this which makes for the hurt and anger and retaliation of insults.

Here is a typical conversation role played again by teenagers:

"You must be stupid buying that L.P. with your Christmas money."
"I'm not stupid. I like the group."
"You are stupid, anyone who spends five pounds on that rubbish has to be."
"Well I'm going round to Barry's now so you won't have to listen to it."
"You're surely not going like that?"
"Like what? What's wrong with me now?"

"You look ridiculous. I wouldn't have been seen dead looking like that when I was your age."

"Well it wasn't the fashion then."

"I don't know what everyone must think of you."

"Look, dad, I don't care what everyone thinks: you're the one who cares. Why don't you leave me alone?"

"Go on, go out to Barry's. I feel sick just looking at you."

"And I can't get out of this house quick enough."

And so it goes on, more hurt piled on more hurt. (You will find the boys discussing this very situation in *Boys Talk*.)

There has to be a difference between values and standards and fashions and tastes. If big issues are made about everything, it is very unlikely that the young person will listen to his or her parents in the really important matters that you are most concerned with.

Too much talking just invites young people to cut off and ignore you. If you then goad them into replying, they will be rude and angry.

It is a time at which the adolescent has difficulty in moderating the voice and controlling the amount of feeling. If he/she chooses to do this by silence, it is unfair to force him/her into arguments.

It is sometimes helpful after an argument to have a cooler look at what was said by both contestants. Usually the degree of hurt makes us turn away from the whole episode and hope that it will go away by the next meeting. If we could understand better what is said, this might help us with our own feelings even if we can't avoid repeating the incidents.

In Kate's book I have explained to her how parents say things which cover a deeper meaning – you can check out some of the 'translations' and see if you recognise them.

Here, it is what the young person says that we must try to understand:

"That's typical – you're prejudiced."	You make general statements about all teenagers: you don't bother to see us as individuals.
"I don't care what everyone thinks."	I only care what you think: I need your approval.

(This is the equivalent of your "I don't care what other people's youngsters do, I only care about you.")

"Why don't you leave me alone?"

I'm trying to be individual, to be myself, not a copy of you. Give me time and I'll get to where you are but it has to be my way.

The communication is the same, but the lines get crossed and the message arrives at the wrong place and time.

7
Sharing responsibility

In the secondary stage of your child's schooling, it is possible that you may again be invited to a meeting to look at a film of sex education.

Usually the parents at this kind of meeting are a mixed group of those who have already seen the film, those who have seen something similar in primary school, those who are confident that their children know everything already, and still some who think their children are not ready for this. They are probably the same group you met in primary school and their attitude hasn't changed.

The important thing, again, is for you to have talked about this with your partner. Know where you are and be absolutely honest about it so that you may help the group or gain help from it.

For example, it is of no help to say, "we don't have any secrets from our children, we discuss everything," when in fact they ask very few questions and so it is easy to discuss what they do bring – if anything. It would be more honest and more helpful to say, "our children don't talk much about sex: should we try to encourage them to do so?"

Again, it is unhelpful and unrealistic if you say, "my children know better than to step out of line – they've been brought up to respect us and obey us." This is a real 'stopper' to any group discussion. It makes everyone else feel so inadequate they dare not open their mouths.

If you do feel tolerably happy with your own family, then you can best help others by hearing what they say and being friendly and sympathetic. Most parents with difficult or problem children fear the censorship of other parents. They avoid coming to parent/ teacher meetings because they are so ashamed of what they feel is an indictment against them as parents.

If you are having a 'difficult' time with your teenagers, then go to these meetings and share your worries, you may be surprised to discover that they are not as awful as you thought.

Some of the discussion may still be about giving factual knowledge to your children. From this age onwards, as already mentioned, it is unlikely that they will ask you direct questions about facts of puberty, intercourse and birth. All this will be better done by the school in the normal course of human biology.

Nevertheless, as a parent it concerns you and you should ask how it is done and how questions are dealt with. It is also useful to know when in the term this will occur so that you may pick up any discussion necessary at home.

The Family as the 'Centre'

If you have read this far you may well be thinking, "what a lot of talk about things that are so obvious. Our grandparents didn't have books to help them, why all this effort on the part of schools, sociologists and counsellors to focus on the importance of relationships."

It would need another book to set out the enormous difference between life as our young people live it today and the life of previous generations. Of course young people since time began have been rebellious, independent, undisciplined, it is part of the pattern of progress. Aggression is a necessary component to ambition.

A twelfth-century historian tells us that young people were never so dissolute, rude and disrespectful of their parents as in that time. No doubt the historian of today will have similar comments to make.

Without entering the sociologists' field and examining the reasons for the changes in society, we do need to remind ourselves of certain basic differences in the structure of family life which has been, till now, the root and source of all relationships.

The family has always been at its greatest strength when it grew and spread in the same environment and community. Children grew up as grandparents grew older. The human chain of aunts and uncles in the vicinity was an everlasting source of unity and security.

Births and deaths were all accepted parts of the richness of the situation. Family visits, family re-unions, weddings, christenings, funerals, were all focal points of the social life.

In this kind of network of relationships, a young person could always find love and tolerance somewhere.

Today's family is more often a small unit of mother, father and possibly two or three children. Statistics show an even smaller average number of children per family.

This little unit will have moved some way from the parental home by the time the first child starts school. It will probably reside in a community of other, similar small units.

In the small family both parents may be working, or mother may work part-time. Children are 'minded' in various ways until old enough to 'mind' themselves. It is not unusual to find young people of eleven and twelve coping with the tea-time part of the day for younger children as well as themselves. They are 'holding the fort' until a parent comes home.

It is not surprising if such a young person, having been given the responsibility of decision-making and caring for younger siblings for part of the day, feels very resentful at being reduced to just another child by the return of a parent.

The situation invites a greater effort at promoting self-discipline and a sense of responsibility in the young person, and at the same time a more humble acknowledgement of our dependency upon this.

This is the situation for the majority of families today. We must also recognise that a considerable number of them are broken units. Here the children may be living with the mother or the father who are separated or divorced. They may, by secondary school, have experienced the second marriage of their parent(s) which means they have adjusted to entirely new relationships with parent-figures and sometimes with half-brothers and half-sisters. They will almost certainly have felt or suppressed great storms of anger, hurt and jealousy which will undoubtedly affect any future sexual relationships they may make.

Added to this we have other one-parent families of either unmarried mothers or young widows or widowers. These little units struggle to give their child a balanced form of relationship, but are very dependent on friends and other families to help give their child a sense of marital relationship.

The environment in which all of this family turmoil is happening is no longer a supporting frame. All the props of social convention, codes of behaviour, moral norms, have been gradually eased out of the structure and we have all to create our own scaffolding to hold our families up. It is not impossible, just a little frightening. You have to keep looking up like a mountaineer — no good looking down: what went before has gone.

What we are looking for are the values that do not change. Each family, because it is a family, has certain basic values that are an inheritance and a legacy for the next generation. Values like honesty, loyalty, concern for others, responsibility: these are all qualities we try to foster in our young. They are at the centre of the books written for your children, *Girls Talk* and *Boys Talk*.

This is what I mean when I talk about the 'centre' of the family. It is not the geographical home: it is the essence of the relationship. It is the core, the heart of the family. It is the centre-point of the relationship from which all flows out and back.

It is something we give our children which they can take anywhere with them, and always find again when they return.

Creating this centre is the life-work of marriage. It begins with the ebb and flow of our own love as married people. Then it catches up each child into this love so that they learn to move happily and freely in it.

It needs to be said that this kind of love is largely the commitment and will to serve and care for and nurture one another. Emotions and feelings of love are some of the ways, but not all of the means by which we achieve this.

One of the essentials for achieving this centre is our own security with ourselves and our situation. It is very easy today to become insecure in our role of parents. We are too easily mesmerised by the vast amount of literature and visual aids on the subject of bringing up our family, as if, from birth to grave, there was a theory and a written answer for every hour of our lives.

What we have to do, as parents, is talk out our own ideas about the pattern and organisation of our family life. Having decided what is best for our particular situation, live it out in confidence that it is right for us. We must not be undermined by the media or the experience of other families. Each family is individual and unique in its relationship. When we accept that and believe it, our children will feel secure.

Nothing is quite so undermining for a young person as to live in an atmosphere of half-expressed uncertainties.

Are you, for instance, an 'if only' parent?

"If only I had more time to be with them . . . ."

"If only I didn't have to go to work . . . ."

"If only their friends weren't allowed out so late."

"If only other people didn't give their children so much pocket money."

"If only their friends didn't swear . . . ."

"If only the school had some discipline."

And so on. If only someone else would make the rules you could be a permanent 'good fairy' granting every wish. It is just not possible. Security for a child is just as much knowing the rules as getting the love.

When you have established the pattern of your home life, then your child will grow up understanding how it works for you and how you all relate. He will recognise other families' patterns, but he will feel secure in his own until he wishes to make his own.

8
Teenage sexuality

The young adult growing up in his or her secondary school is still going to present you with plenty of opportunities for giving additional knowledge on the subject of sex and relationships.

If the communication is pretty good you will have no difficulty in recognising the opportunity, but you may still have difficulties in coping with the answers. On the other hand your teenager may be shy, reticent or reluctant to admit to his or her thoughts about some subjects to do with sexuality.

In that case your problem is 'spotting' the question – and then giving back information in a sufficiently casual way that the young person will not become embarrassed.

Some of the things young people discuss today are subjects that you have not thought about in any depth. If you have accepted certain attitudes, for example, towards sexual behaviour or abortion, because you were brought up in those ideas by *your* family, a challenge from your teenager can leave you standing on one leg and saying "well, I disagree". This is not very helpful and does not make for useful discussion.

That is why it is good sometimes to talk about these things to your partner and with friends and at school meetings. It broadens your view and gives you practice in saying what you think. It is not a question of capitulating your principles or proving other people wrong; it is really learning to listen and hear someone else without emotional prejudice. If we feel too strongly about something, it blots out all reasonable discussion.

The reason questions become more complicated in the adolescent stage of development is partly because of the personal emotional involvement of the young person with the subject, partly because the question often has a moral content.

It is no longer a simple question like "how does the baby get into the tummy?" but, "how does a girl get pregnant if she is not married?" And when you think you've answered that one correctly, you discover that what they really meant is "why didn't she use a contraceptive?"

It is helpful in clarifying the problem to take each part of a question and check out first of all what the young persons themselves know or think the answer is.

When you have given the factual part of the answer, like explaining what an abortion is, you can then deal with how various people feel about this matter and what your views are on the subject. Be sure to listen to what the questioner is saying and don't be so anxious to get his agreement that you don't hear his anxiety.

Every time you are asked about the moral aspect of a situation be sure to separate the person involved from the situation. This avoids any possible hurt to friends or their families about whom you may not know.

For example, everyone accepts that stealing is wrong. It is punished in school and it is punished in law. If a person steals because he is desperate, or his family is starving, or he needs help in some way, we feel sympathy and understanding for that person, but we cannot say that therefore stealing is right. We can only say there were special circumstances that caused him or her to do this. It is the circumstances which must be changed, not the law.

Masturbation

One of the subjects which worry boys is that of masturbation. You may get a direct question, "What is masturbation?" from a young or rather innocent type of youngster, but he is much more likely to be too embarrassed to ask it.

He has probably heard boys talking about this in school and thinks he's missing out on something. Often, if he has not discovered this for himself, he will mispronounce the word. This gives the reluctant parent a chance to misunderstand and avoid explaining and it makes the boy feel a fool.

Never – it is the largest never in the book of sex – make anyone 'feel a fool' either by words or behaviour or tone of voice when you are dealing with matters of sex. The subject is too intimate and the young adolescent is too vulnerable.

The indirect question about this may be a boy describing some behaviour he has seen in the school lavatories. Or you may suspect it from his own behaviour when you go into his room to say goodnight.

By the way, are you still keeping up this habit of saying goodnight? A last check all round before going to bed yourself will often surprise a few secret tears or a wide-awake worrying youngster. Many a heavy heart has emptied its woe into the pillow in the small hours. Night-time often finds a teenager at his most unguarded. In bed he feels young and 'mothered' again and it is a good time for getting 'close' to feelings.

However the chance comes, you should take it in order to allay his fears. Many young boys feel masturbation is wrong, and yet because it is so pleasurable they are confused. It is probably the first time that they face the idea that sexual pleasure can also carry bad feelings if it is not an appropriate situation or relationship.

The guilt can be lessened by your matter-of-fact treatment of the subject. Lots of boys, probably most, have masturbated at some time; it is pleasurable and it discharges some of the pressure from the build up of sperm. It does not cause any physical harm or prevent them from having proper sexual intercourse.

On the other hand you must recognise that usually the boy's own instinctive feelings are not exactly of pride in the matter. Why else would boys whisper and hide the fact like a secret? It is more helpful to acknowledge his feelings and move him on to positive thinking, dismissing the idea of guilt and assuring him that his new-found powers will make more sense in the context of future marriage. The love that is still growing in him will turn outwards towards someone he can love more than himself and the sexual act will have its proper completion which at present is only being hinted at in masturbation.

In *Boys Talk* there is a more detailed discussion of this on a boy's level. It is not included in *Girls Talk* because in all the years that I have worked in relationships and sex education, I have only twice been asked by girls to explain what masturbation means. That is not to say that girls don't masturbate or that they all know about it anyway. It is quite simply not the problem for girls that it is for boys and therefore not necessary information unless sought for by the girls.

Girls do not get the same build up of sexual tension that a boy gets. There is less instinctive need to release the tension. They do not get physical change under tension, like a boy getting an erection. Boys have to handle their penis to pass water, whereas there is almost no contact apart from bathing that a girl needs to make with her sex organs. Masturbation for a girl is something which she learns, rather than happening by chance, and she is in control of the situation herself.

9
Some difficult topics

Homosexuality

Boys and girls seem to become aware of this form of sexuality at very early ages. Almost before any understanding of the real meaning of the word they express with giggles and nudges their awareness of some implicit homosexual relationship between two boys or two girls.

All the normal developing of friendship through relationships with one of their own sex has become distorted and it seems that, sadly, the young cannot give themselves permission to enjoy one another's company naturally.

It is difficult to assign blame anywhere in particular for this. Perhaps it is the price paid for trying to bring some normality to the lives of those who are genuine homosexuals.

It is worthwhile picking this up and discussing it more than once with your children if the opportunity arises. There are more questions in this than just "what does it mean?"

They should be able to understand that the majority of people are heterosexual, that is, able to fall in love with someone of the opposite sex, get married and have a family. A homosexual, however, does not feel this kind of love towards the opposite sex; he or she would much rather be married to one of their own sex.

Children of every age have a strong built-in concept of the family as being a man and a woman and children. They can readily accept that anything else is a deviation from the normal. As they grow older, the problem is in their desire to be ever-tolerant and ever-accepting of every kind of behaviour because such openness is supposed to separate youth from old age, which is another word for all of us. In fact, grandparents are quite good at showing the young that tolerance is often a virtue of old age – it goes with wisdom.

In adolescence, then, the question is more likely to be "why?" and "is it wrong?" There is also some anxiety around that they may be 'that kind of person'. These ideas are vastly encouraged by the media which focus so much attention on homosexual groups in plays, stories, books, articles, documentaries, that it is not surprising if young people think that heterosexuals are a small minority of people.

However, such plays and documentaries do result in some of the best discussions I have had in schools on this subject. If you are watching such a programme in your home, open out the discussion. Don't kill it with statements like "What rubbish!" It gives you a good chance to check out where your child is in these matters and correct any misunderstandings.

The question "why?" may be to do with hormones and in their own book they can read about which hormones produce manly attributes and which ones make the feminine attributes. It is not difficult for them to understand that if these were not functioning properly, it would change the nature of the person.

There are other reasons like hereditary factors and relationships in childhood which can affect the development of the sexuality of a person. As a rule young people do not understand these explanations – neither do many parents manage to explain. There are authentic sources of information about this to which the young person may be directed if old enough to pursue the matter.

The probability of them being anxious about themselves is a necessary piece of discussion. If you are not sure that they are asking for that reason, it is still worthwhile reassuring them that young people of their age are still developing their own sexuality.

Explain that during adolescence it is quite normal and quite usual for young people to make close friends with people of their own sex. Both boys and girls can get quite attached to older men or women, like teachers or friends of their parents, and feel almost 'in love' with them. It is the beginning of understanding a different kind of love from that which they feel towards parents or 'group' friends, but it is not a fully developed sexual love.

For most people, sexual love develops towards people of their own age and of the opposite sex, with the prospect of marriage and the foundation of a new family. The homosexual finds it impossible to develop in this way.

So on the point of right or wrong, it is best to explain that homosexuality is neither right nor wrong; it is a state of being. If they meet someone with a physical handicap, once they have got over the stage of looking and being surprised, they are sympathetic and helpful. In just the same way they might be surprised and curious about a homosexual, but once they accept him or her they can be friendly and natural.

It is also useful to point out that a person who is physically handicapped does not want to be treated as 'special' — he is insistent that you accept him as he is and behave normally and naturally with him. The same rule applies with personality handicaps. You must be natural yourself and act in the way that is normal to your nature.

Boys are more likely to worry about this than girls. They hear more talk among older boys and young men than girls do. They are thrown together, by the design of our public lavatories, with all kinds of men, and sometimes they feel quite threatened by this. Whilst it is reassuring for them to know and understand what a genuine homosexual is, they still need to be warned about undesirable strangers who may approach them for improper reasons. They should always mention this to you or a teacher, and discuss what should be done, so that it does not become a buried secret.

Rape

If boys worry more about homosexuals, then girls certainly worry more about rape. Why shouldn't they? The press frequently reports these incidents. Girls are warned from childhood never to take a lift or a gift from any stranger. The police visit schools, show films of pick-ups and talk to youngsters about these dangers. Still it happens, still there are young people who think they can decide whether a man seems kind or trustworthy.

You need to explain that rape is a very violent thing and very harmful to a girl. People who commit these crimes are usually sick in the mind. A girl must never put herself in a situation where such a person could harm her. That is why you are so anxious if she comes home late, and why you need to know where she is and who she is with. Always make your daughters decide how they are getting home and with whom, before they go out in the evening. Girls frequently tell me that they hate it when dad picks them up after a disco, but they are quite glad to know he is coming! Such an ambiguous feeling is understandable at that age, so just make up your minds to suffer the protests and settle for your own peace of mind.

Trial Marriage?

"Do you believe in trial marriage, Miss?" is a favourite discussion-starter among teenager groups. On the whole they seem to think it is a pretty good idea. They might even say this at home in the form of a statement like "I think trial marriages are a good idea" – and wait for your reaction.

They have not thought too much about marriage; it's really the permanence of it that frightens them. A trial marriage for a boy usually means he doesn't see himself tied up for ever and this gives him an escape. For a girl it may be that she is afraid of the sexual part of marriage; she thinks she may not like it and this will give her an escape.

Many children see all around them evidence of marriages that were mistakes or changed after a few years and fell apart. They are quite seriously afraid of making these mistakes themselves.

For all these reasons it is better not to jump in with a moralistic approach. Allow them to say what they are thinking and explore with them some of the implications. In a group the boys learn from the girls that there is no way they would consider living with a boy unless he really loves her. Since love is not measured in time, it is always seen as 'for ever'. So it is only a theory that you could put it on 'trial': the reality of that situation is that either it will last for ever, in which case you may as well get married, or you know at the start that it won't last for ever, in which case why begin?

In this type of discussion there is an opportunity to talk about the differences in make-up of boys and girls. Most girls have a great need to love and feel loved before they can become aroused sexually. Boys, however, can get aroused sexually in a mechanistic way without involvement of deep feelings. Pornography has a much greater appeal to boys. The now customary nude pictures in papers, magazines and films can switch them on pretty quickly. Proximity to an attractive girl can get them sexually interested, but there is no deep love in any of these incidents.

You should find a way of telling your young man (or men) that this is a simple biological fact about boys and men. They must, in recognising and acknowledging this, also accept that it is not so for a girl. There must be a tender and loving approach with all girls in the matters of sexual behaviour, even if it is only for a goodnight kiss. If you can help them to understand this when they are young they will become much better lovers when they are husbands.

Similarly, when talking to daughters about men you should point out that boys are 'switched-on' much more quickly than they are. This puts the onus on them, to a certain degree, to be honest about

71

stating the 'terms' of the friendship. It is unfair for a girl to appear to be offering invitations for sexual advances and then to be 'innocent' and indignant with the boy when he wants to go beyond kissing and holding hands.

If she does not signal clearly where her boundaries lie she is not being honest with a boy. If she does not set limits as to what she will allow in petting, then she teaches him nothing about the value of love and of herself as a woman. The girl who allows any kind of behaviour as acceptable is telling a young man that this is what a girl expects.

If she sets limits and the boy friend 'cools off' her, it may make her heart ache a little but she has only lost someone who wanted her body. There has to be more than that in a friendship. If the friendship is wanted and enjoyed, both girl and boy will respect the wishes of the other in the matter of sexual behaviour.

If the boy moves on to press his attentions on another girl, then even if he succeeds in getting what he wants from her, at least the first girl will have taught him that everyone is different. He will know that some girls have very definite views about the importance of sexual relationships.

This is a unique decision that each girl must make but she cannot make it unless she gets very clear supportive messages from you about what you think is appropriate behaviour for the situation.

Teenagers and intercourse

Here is a transcript from a discussion with 15/16-year-olds:

"I think it's a good idea to get sexual experience before getting married."

"So do I. You might find you don't fit sexually."

"What does that mean?"

"Well, some people are sexually incompatible. You know: they don't enjoy it."

"That's stupid, it's not all that important in marriage."

"Oh yes it is. It's what you get married for."

"Well if you have it first without getting married then you needn't get married for it, need you?"

"I want to be a virgin when I'm married."

"I don't. I want to be good at it."

"Well I'd like to be experienced, but I want to marry a virgin."

"So how are you going to get experienced? Who wants your second-hand goods?"

"Nobody is a virgin these days, it's old-fashioned."

"If you stayed a virgin, when you got married wouldn't you want your husband to be the same?"

"No, I should like him to know how to make love to me."

"I wouldn't mind if I wasn't a virgin, we would both start equal."

That kind of conversation is often the beginning of a serious discussion in which counsellor or group leader helps them to examine these statements and work out what the reality is all about.

It is unlikely that in your homes you would receive the full weight of all that in one conversation, but a lot of the anxieties underlying the statements are present in all young people. They may express it to you in terms of "a girl (or boy) in my school says. . . ." or "do you think people behave like that?" after watching a film on television where everyone gets in and out of everyone else's bed.

It might then be helpful to look at some of the meanings behind the words.

The young people in our dialogue – and most others – have been influenced by the amount of so-called informed opinion on the subject of sexual expertise which appears in women's magazines, popular press and even the teenage periodicals. Emphasis is always on the necessity for giving a 'good performance' and the implication is that no one will want to marry them if they don't come up to 'A-level' standard.

The whole of that conversation is really about being afraid that they won't reach the expectation of the person they marry.

It is best to approach these attitudes, as parents, from the strength of your own loving experience. Do not be afraid in these areas to give your own witness because if you have already established a sufficiently good relationship for this kind of discussion to arise, then your children will respect what you offer as your own experience of life.

It must be offered humbly as your conviction and not arrogantly as a dictation to them.

What you want them to understand is that their adolescence is a learning time, a school for sexuality. Instead of rushing into the examination at the end of the course, they should use the time to find out all they can about themselves and other people so that the choice of partner will ensure total happiness, not just success in certain areas of the relationship.

If, when they come to this choice, they have exercised some control over their sexual behaviour, they will have a deeper relationship to be explored in marriage.

Intercourse is one part of a total relationship. If you practise that part, why not a test in cooking or mending? And if you fail at any of these, will you stop loving each other, or do you intend starting to love each other after passing the test? In real terms of relationship it simply cannot be divided up and examined. The whole of the marriage relationship is the living together, not at any particular time or place or circumstance but always, everywhere, in health and morning sickness, in hopes of promotion or despair or unemployment, until death tears you apart – and even then to die a little with that person.

Young people, because they are young and without experience, have only a theoretical idea about intercourse. They are completely surprised by the revelation that it can have many meanings within the context of marriage. It can create love or life, it can be peaceful or comforting, it can be searching or anxious, it can be asking or answering, it can be forgiving or atoning, it can be tender or aggressive, it can be joyful, thankful, affirming and even funny. It only takes on a meaning in the security of marriage.

At the end of the teenagers' discussion, these same young people were saying:

"I suppose I've never really seriously thought about this before, I just said what I've heard other people say."

"I would like to be special and just loved by one person, but if you say that, everyone laughs at you."

"I just talk about all this sex and experience because everyone else does."

"Really everyone just wants a normal happy marriage. It's just not exciting to talk about."

"My mother and father met when they were sixteen and they are still happy and always joking with each other."

"I don't feel so scared now we've talked about it. I think if you really love someone and they really love you, all the other things would just work out."

Teenage mums

"A girl in our school has left because she's having a baby." This could be a statement of fact or a question. Whichever it is, it is inviting a response, otherwise it would not have been made.

It needs to be checked out from two points of view. Is the young person asking you how this happens if the girl is not married? That might be a young child's question. Is he or she asking you to show your attitude to this situation? That would be an adolescent question.

Some kind of mild response like "these things do happen" gives them a safe space to put another question. If they don't, you could follow up with something about the plight of the baby. A young mother alone without any father to help has a real struggle to keep her baby. The responsibility is often too great. She has not had enough time in her young life to be carefree and happy. After the novelty of the baby is gone, she wants freedom again and the poor little thing is neglected or passed over to other members of the family, such as grandparents.

Why it happens to young girls is because they have not thought about these things seriously. You have talked quite a lot to your child(ren) and bought them a book to help think about these matters. But some young people have never had this chance. It may be that they are irresponsible, or thoughtless, or angry about their lives at home and looking for some comfort elsewhere.

If such a person meets up with someone of the opposite sex who is equally thoughtless, then they may arrive at this situation. Because they think of sex as a fun thing, nothing to do with loving, they may fool about, petting and exciting one another until they have no more control left and find themselves having intercourse. If they are lonely or unhappy this also might bring them into a situation where they try to get love from each other by intercourse. For whatever reason, it is rare that a loving situation suitable for marriage will be the outcome.

Usually the boy is appalled by this sudden responsibility and the possibility of being tied down for a lifetime. His fears kill any feeling he might have had for the girl and he leaves her to her own problem. The girl (you have already done your homework on how she needs love to survive a sexual experience) feels abandoned and utterly miserable, however brave a face she may show to her friends.

These are simple facts which your children should hear from you at the earliest opportunity — and it is easy enough to find an introduction to this subject from documentaries or plays on television, or straight out of the neighbourhood news book.

If it is attitude they are looking for, you need to make it clear that it is one of those situations where you must separate your feelings for the person from what is actually done. What you are saying to them is that although you think it is wrong to bring a child into the world without thought and planning, both the mother and the child will still need help.

The child is completely innocent about the whole situation and that is why society has changed its attitude to one of kindness and sympathy. The child needs to be loved and he can only get that love from the mother. She can only give love if she feels loved. That is why we try to help and love the young mother so that she can nurture her child. But however much it may appear that society no longer frowns upon the unmarried mother, this is only a front. Behind every young girl's pregnancy is a tale of hurt and shame and misery for the whole family involved. Most girls know this if they have heard their parents discuss the subject.

Many girls have said to me, "My parents would never turn me out but it would break their hearts." Others say, "My dad says he'd see me through it but he'd never feel the same again about me." "I'd never let it happen to me, I wouldn't want to hurt my parents."

These are all responsible statements which show that young people can make the right response if their parents will discuss these matters. You must have enough trust in your children to share your feelings about these matters.

It is a temptation to concentrate on the girls with this subject and by implication to suggest it is less important for the boy. This is quite wrong if we are trying to build values out of relationships. The boy must be responsible for seeing that he does not bring about this kind of unhappiness. We must have an expectation from him as well as from our daughters. To be in control of yourself and your situation is a goal for any youngster, boy or girl, and it is certainly a manly attribute to be taught to our sons.

Contraception

The kind of discussion I have just described often leads adolescents into a discussion about the use of contraceptives.

A younger child of junior school age might ask you what a contraceptive is, because he has heard the word. It only requires for him a simple answer like: "It is something which a mother and father use to prevent the sperm meeting the ovum when they want to be sure they won't start a baby growing. It is small and fits over the penis or inside the vagina. There is also a pill to take; it has the same effect."

The older child probably has a fair knowledge of what they are either from hearing talk about them or reading about them. His question is again centred around attitude. He wants to know why young people don't use contraceptives to prevent the girl getting pregnant.

That kind of question needs some manoeuvring, depending on your own attitudes about this. The question presupposes that you think young people should be allowed to have intercourse. That has to be dealt with first before tackling the corollary to it.

I have already indicated lines upon which the subject of intercourse outside of marriage could be discussed. If this kind of attitude is given by you they would probably accept your answer that contraceptives wouldn't be needed if intercourse didn't take place. If they don't accept that attitude from you, then they will probably take the question elsewhere like school and sound out a few teachers.

But you should not be discouraged when they appear to turn down your values or standards. Provided your communication has always been good, the values will still reside in them. What happens quite often is that they wish to test them with other people. They may not be able to take them into their own thinking until they have 'chosen' them for themselves.

Values are like religion – and very related. Few young people today will accept their parents' religion unquestioningly. They have to deny it first so that they can take it up as really being their own belief.

If parents could understand that, and have trust in their children, it would facilitate that part of their growing up. Unfortunately parents become afraid and anxious when they see established family patterns being challenged. They make angry noises and loud declarations and end up alienating the young person in a particular way so that he cannot get back to a discussion point.

Abortion

Here is the beginning of a discussion with 14-year-olds on the subject of abortion:

"I disagree with it, it's murder."
"No it isn't. It depends on the circumstances."
"Would you want to have the baby if you had been raped?"
"I'm talking about normal things like school girls getting pregnant."
"Well they shouldn't get pregnant."
"It would be better to get rid of it than ruin their lives."
"My parents wouldn't let me."
"My parents would pay for me."
"I wouldn't let my parents decide."

Here, at the start of the conversation, as frequently happens, a number of confused attitudes arise. They are confused because they are partly a reflection of what they have heard from other people and partly their own inability to see clearly the issues.

It is a good example of how our feelings for a person in a certain situation cannot be allowed to confuse our attitude to an action taken.

You may feel quite open yourself on the whole subject in which case you must present a fair explanation of the facts of abortion, as well as discussing possible reasons for permitting an abortion. You may on the other hand have strong definite views that it is wrong and you wish to hand these attitudes onto your child. You will accomplish whatever you want more easily by exploring what your child already knows about the subject and what feelings they have towards the idea.

You could be surprised to find that what they have heard from friends at school, and what they have learnt about the growth of a baby in the womb, is sufficient for them to have made up their own minds that it is wrong. By hearing this from your son or daughter you are spared your own explanations about attitudes. Everything you say will be an endorsement of their views.

If, however, they have heard in their peer group about people in desperate circumstances, or read of some sad case in the newspaper about a battered wife who finds herself pregnant, then you need to talk these cases out individually.

Central to the argument is the unborn child. Do they think a baby is a person from the moment of conception? If they do and if they think abortion is killing that person, then the crime remains the same whatever the circumstances. Like the example of stealing, we feel sympathy and concern for the person affected, but cannot therefore say killing is right.

People who believe abortion is not wrong usually hold the argument that a baby is not a person until it has a separate life from the mother. If they want to talk from that point they must consider how an expectant mother feels about her unborn baby.

In *Girls Talk* Kate sees very clearly that for her aunt the baby was very real right from the start. As parents yourselves you are best equipped to tell your children how you felt about your babies, how they move and turn, and make themselves very real to you during the pregnancy.

In China a baby born starts his second year of life: he is called one year old – which seems to say something about the reality of the unborn child.

The baby is real: there is no doubt. He could survive prematurely, if he had to. It is the attitude of the parents that is the deciding factor. If you want a baby he lives for you from the day of conception. But if you don't want the baby and intend to have an abortion, or even entertain the possibility, then you cannot allow yourself to think in terms of a person: it would make it too difficult to see it through.

It is significant that people who favour abortions talk about embryos and foetuses whereas the happy expectant mother talks about her 'baby'.

Other Facts

There are still quite a number of factual questions that your young family may put to you at various times. Most of these are to do with daily situations that arise.

Handicapped children are the result of imperfect life cells, or may have suffered a severe illness or accident at or near birth. There is nothing we can do to prevent this – medical science does not yet know enough to correct the course of development. Research goes on continually to help parents who have handicapped children and to advise those who may have a hereditary likelihood of having a handicapped child.

Young people will hear quite a lot about smoking and drinking, and also about taking drugs. They may discuss this with you and no doubt you will endorse the school's teaching on the dangers of these, both to them as adolescents and later to their offspring.

There are posters and warnings about V.D. in many public places and most schools offer some explanation on this subject also. It is something I have not mentioned in either the girls' or the boys' book because it seems contradictory to aim your teaching at the value of love and good relationships and then to warn them about diseases which are usually contracted from promiscuous sexual relationships.

However, if your children ask you what it is, you would need to tell them that these are serious diseases of the sexual organs that need clinical treatment. You could add later in the conversation that these diseases are usually caught by sexual intercourse or close sexual contact with someone who is already infected. There are plenty of leaflets with suitable explanations in most clinics.

Non-identical twins

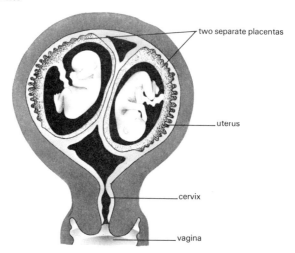

two separate placentas

uterus

cervix

vagina

Identical twins

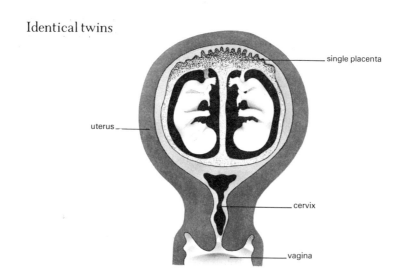

single placenta

uterus

cervix

vagina

How twins are formed and the difference between identical twins and non-identical is a subject of interest. Opposite is a simple diagram to show how both kinds of twins grow in the womb.

You can see that although each baby floats in its own sac of water, the identical twins feed and live from one placenta, but non-identical feed and live from separate placentae.

Most of these facts I have dealt with in more detail in the girls' and boys' books where they are answered in language appropriate for their age. If you read these books it is easier for you to adapt the language to suit what seems natural for you. The important thing, as always, is the natural ease with which you deal with the question.

Many questions we are asked are quite searching, requiring specific medical or biological knowledge. There is no reason why we should have every answer at our finger tips. Few people would mind looking a word up in a dictionary for their child in order to give them an exact and accurate definition. It is just as normal to look up answers of this nature in a medical book or encyclopedia.

Adoption

Some parents in school discussion groups mention that they have adopted children and feel that this presents a difficulty in dealing with sex education.

All of the facts that are discussed here are relevant to any child. The difficulty is perhaps more in the parent than the child. The parent is describing a process of pregnancy and birth which they feel did not actually occur to them. However, they did occur for your child and that is the focus of your explanation.

Even with natural parents the facts are usually explained in a fairly objective fashion like talking about 'the mother's womb': it is very rare that we say "I" or "we".

When the adopted child is young, he is usually content with the knowledge that you love him enough to want him for your child. The rest of his questions are just factual like any child's. It is in adolescence with the awakening search for identity that the adopted child's question, "who am I?", is much more complicated than the natural child's.

The sudden and hitherto unknown feelings of anger or depression or frustration will cause him to wonder if it is some strange inheritance from an unknown past. Parents will wonder also if this is normal because they may not have a source of reference in other children. It may be their first experience of bringing up adolescent youngsters. If they both get into a situation where they are frightened by these feelings, they may say hurtful and incredible things to each other which seem to make or confirm this sense of being with strangers.

Each child and parent/child situation is so different and unique it is not possible to give out general rules to be applied for the alleviation of pain.

However, some reassurance can be given. Parents of adopted children should talk to other parents as much as possible, especially in these school situations where there is help available to them. They will find out that most teenagers are reacting in the same way as theirs to the present situation. They are poised for flight at the slightest provocation!

From the young persons' point of view, they need lots of reassurance that they are normal. The feeling of being 'different' is somehow heightened at this insecure time and they may become very introspective.

In the course of school counselling, I have talked to many adopted teenagers. They are very protective towards their adopted parents. They express anxieties that they might hurt these people in some way and they don't want to because they have been so good to them. The fear can easily be understood. The natural child has a certain security of tenure in the family – he is so sure of himself that he can shout "I hate you" to his parents and still be sure of their love. The adopted child wants to give vent to this feeling as well, but is very afraid of how hurt they may be and not at all sure how he can climb back into the relationship.

Another problem with adopted children is whether they will or won't go in search of their real parents. They are very ambiguous about these feelings, sensing that there is some hidden danger in this of more hurt – but for whom?

They frequently try to escape from these problems by turning their ideas towards careers that would virtually remove all parents and just provide parent-figures. They think about going into the navy or army or police force — both girls and boys say this. Girls also talk about living in a nurses' home or working in a hotel where they can live in, or working in a children's home. After the turmoil of adolescence has passed these ideas usually pass also and the young adult settles gratefully into the warmth of the family once more.

Meanwhile all the parent can do is be there, be accepting and be patient. Have faith that the relationship you built from childhood is stronger and more real than the teenager's flight into imaginary rediscovered relationships.

If your child wants to know why his mother abandoned him, he or she can be helped to see that the mother never really knew him so she didn't feel she was abandoning a person like he is now; she was abandoning a situation that she couldn't cope with. A baby was part of that situation.

It is more likely that she gave him up for adoption because she wanted more for him than she was able to give. She may have had no home, no father to support him and out of love made the decision to let him be adopted. There is always a lot of sadness about these things at the time but it passes because people must go on living. Hopefully she has found some other happiness and likes to think of him as being happy.

It is unlikely that she would want him back now. She might feel curious to know how he looked and grew up, but she couldn't live all her life wanting him back: it would be too difficult. So she has to put him out of her mind and concentrate on her present life.

It may not be necessary to talk about that possibility with your child, but because of the changed laws regarding information about the parents of adopted children, it is worth your while thinking how you would discuss this.

One-parent families are in a very similar kind of situation. Usually it is a mother-and-child family and eventually the child is going to ask about the father. It is better to think this out very early when the child is only a baby. Some parents who think they will wait to see how it arises are suddenly asked when they least expect it and are trapped into giving an answer which they later regret.

You cannot take back the initial shock of a painfully-learnt piece of information. For the sake of the child it is necessary to sacrifice what bitterness may be there. Give your child the comfort of knowing that daddy did love her very much: that is how she was born – because you loved each other. Why he left you is something you need to work out in a positive way. Perhaps he was too young and thought he would be no good as a father. Perhaps there were other people he had to look after. Little children will often accept a simple "I don't know", for they know that there are things we don't know. It is older ones who think we should know everything.

The important thing in this situation will be your voice and attitude. If you are warm and compassionate about the situation, she or he will have warm feelings towards men even without a father-figure. If you sound bitter or angry she or he will become timid and untrusting with men.

The child is unlikely to grow up deprived of men, but you can make efforts to cultivate friends where she or he can feel at home in a family atmosphere and enjoy sharing somebody's dad.

The sex-information part of the upbringing is no different because you are the only parent. All the biological facts remain the same. It is just the relationship side that requires a little more thought and planning.

As a general rule the single parent works very hard at these relationships. Because they have been alone a great deal with the little child, they have become very close indeed. Children from single-parent families have said to me "I'm very close to my mother: we can talk about anything".

Divorced parents

Many children today have lived through the turmoil of a divorce. Many have had to adjust to a new parent and new half-brothers and half-sisters. All these situations take a great deal of courage and a complete renewal of faith in the relationships.

Here again, there is no problem in the information side of sex-education. There is often the opportunity of sharing in the arrival of a new baby in the family. Young children from the second marriage may join the others, so there is a wider circle of relationships in which to learn.

On the other hand there is more frustration and anger than usual and also a fair amount of jealousy to contend with. These factors make it harder for the parents at a time when they themselves are recovering from trauma or discovering new relationships.

The questions that perplex the young mind are whether the departed parent loves them. Why should they be left behind? Is it their fault? It is necessary here also to try and get rid of bitterness and anger before attempting to answer these questions.

Keep your focus on the child and remember always that everything you say and the attitude you show in the area of sexual relationships will be taken by your children into their marriage.

It is also necessary for you to work on yourself and come to some peaceful acceptance of your own situation, however hard it may be, so that you can convey attitudes of love and sympathy to your child.

Always make it clear that you married in love and that was how you thought it would stay − and that the children were born in this time of loving. It is only now that it seems to have been a mistake and you are no longer happy living together, but that hasn't changed the love for the children. Men and women love each other in a different way from the love they give their children. When a father and mother are arguing about something it doesn't change their feelings towards their children. It may not seem like comfort for an unhappy child, but wounds heal, and are better healed with tears than with bitterness.

There are good counselling agencies available to help families with relationship difficulties. It is well worth getting help in the early days of separation or divorce, to sort your own feelings out and work through your own anger − it will help you to be a more compassionate parent for your child's sake.

Unmarried mothers faced with bringing up their child would also benefit from counselling.

A lot of people think marriage counsellors are only interested in mending marriages. Their real interest is in mending people. They can help individuals to be fuller happier people who can get more pleasure than they knew was possible from their lives.

If you want more personal counselling in family relationships, then you should get in touch with the local marriage guidance centres, who have trained counsellors available to help in any kind of relationship difficulty.

Anorexia Nervosa

All too often this potentially serious illness is dismissed in conversation as one of the follies of too much slimming. The medical profession is still learning about the causes, symptoms and treatments. One thing emerges clearly from studies made so far: the illness occurs in deeply unhappy young people, usually girls, with a very poor image of themselves. They cannot imagine anyone wanting them for their own sake. The dieting syndrome is just a part of the "make myself more attractive" drive. If that were all there was to it, then the slimmer would stop because she achieves the desired weight loss and everyone admires her for it. But the objective is not so simple: it is part of an unsatisfied need to control her life: success in controlling the bodily appetite gives such a sense of power over self that the anorectic is afraid to relinquish her dieting.

Every case is individual and unique. This makes it impossible to give a blueprint for checking out your child. It is a 'creeping' illness whose onset is slow but in which the mind and spirit and body are all attacked at the same time. It is of no use to treat the body separately from the troubled mind. Even if the patient gains in weight and appears to be eating, the cure is not effective unless there is a change in her spirit. She must have a wish to be cured, a motive for living a better life, an improved image of herself.

They are all people who need counselling over quite a long period. Many young people come home from hospital, apparently pronounced cured, but if there is no follow-up of care and counselling, they will almost certainly relapse into the illness.

Most of the cases studied have shown that the girls concerned have been intelligent 'middle class' young people with too high expectations from themselves or their parents, especially in academic attainment. They come in the age range thirteen to twenty-one.

Their background shows a high proportion of turmoil and argument in the home: statistics suggest that 40 per cent of anorectics have parents separated or threatening to do so, and another 41 per cent of parents are exhibiting sexual problems in the home. It is hardly surprising that the young person finds it hard to 'grow up', to separate herself from this parental image.

This book is not concerned with diagnosis or treatment. The illness requires expert medical attention. The area of involvement here is to do with the relationships. The whole illness is rooted in the relationships which still exist (or which ought to but do not exist) for the patient.

Your degree of communication, the way in which you work at all the aspects of relationship with your children, is their protection against this illness. It is also your promise to the next generation that their parents will be reasonably stable emotionally, and able to live complete and happy sexual lives. However, we cannot always put our finger on the anxieties of our children, so we need to be aware of some of the pointers.

Slimming during the growth time of adolescence is not a good idea. If your daughter is very self-conscious about being too fat then she should talk to her doctor about it. It is better to reassure her that most young people are attractive just because they are young and good to look at. By the time they leave school, they have grown into pretty nice shapes.

If that line is not effective then she may become depressed. This could be accompanied by anxiety about school work, exams, meeting people. She may become quiet, withdrawn, non-communicative. She may lose her appetite, or refuse to eat, or eat secretly. If all that gets out of hand there will be a severe weight loss.

If you are still not getting the message, the next sign will be the menstrual periods will stop. It is usually this which will eventually take a parent to the doctor with her daughter. This weight loss and missing of periods is a very serious matter. It is not sufficient for the girl to be given some kind of drug to 'help' the depression. She needs proper attention for anorexia and the parent should be sure that all the tests are made to diagnose the trouble. If you are not satisfied with the progress of your daughter, you should consult her school.

The school doctor will certainly take the matter seriously and so will the staff, who will help in building self-esteem, encouraging friendships and lifting some of the burden of work.

Do not try to cope alone with this problem: if you do, you will find the illness controls you as well as your daughter. Moreover, she can use it to obtain her own ends, though the struggle to control is part of the illness, not a personal attack on you. Find a good counselling service in your area and obtain all the help you can for you and your daughter. You could well write to: Anorexia Aid H.Q., Gravel House, Copthall Corner, Chalfont St Peter, Bucks.

*   *   *

There is no conclusion to personal relationships. The richness you give of this to your children, they will in turn give to theirs. The redemption of the human race depends on this constant cycle of affirmation in which we love, forgive and recreate one another.